Lime Green Chair

Lime Green Chair

Chris Andrews

WAYWISER

First published in 2012 by

THE WAYWISER PRESS

Bench House, 82 London Road, Chipping Norton, Oxon OX7 5FN, UK
P.O. Box 6205, Baltimore, MD 21206, USA
http://waywiser-press.com

Editor-in-Chief
Philip Hoy

Senior American Editor
Joseph Harrison

Associate Editors
Eric McHenry Clive Watkins Greg Williamson

Copyright © Chris Andrews, 2012

The right of Chris Andrews to be identified as the author of this work
has been asserted by him in accordance with the
Copyright, Designs and Patents Act of 1988.

All rights reserved

A CIP catalogue record for this book is available from the British Library

ISBN 978-1-904130-51-2

Printed and bound by
T.J. International Ltd., Padstow, Cornwall, PL28 8RW

for Michelle

Acknowledgements

I would like to thank the editors of the magazines, newspapers and anthologies in which some of these poems first appeared, sometimes in different versions: *The Age*: "Rooms", "Megalomania", "Zombie Charmers", "A Theory of Next Thursday Night", "Mottoes"; *Antipodes*: "If I Stop", "Lost and Found", "Late Extras"; *The Australian*: "Tourism (II)"; *Australian Book Review*: "By Accident", "Invisible Hinges", "Both Hands"; *Australian Literary Review*: "If I Start", "On Earth As It Is; *The Best Australian Poems 2007*: "Both Hands"; *The Best Australian Poems 2008*: "A Different Party"; *The Best Australian Poems 2010:* "By Accident*"; The Best Australian Poems 2011*: "Function Centre"; *Blast*: "Far Call", "As Le Tellier Says", "Function Centre"; *Buzz*: "Kitchen in Transit", "Continuous Screening"; *Eureka Street*: "My Life without You", "This Way Up"; *Famous Reporter*: "Envoy"; *Heat*: "The Same Party", "A Different Party", "The Mist Lifts", "As Parra Says"; *Island*: "Weather Break"; *London Review of Books*: "Nap"; *The Manchester Review*: "Tourism (I)," "Name Dropping"; *The Night Road* (Newcastle Poetry Prize Anthology 2009): "Burnt Umbrella"; *Stride Magazine*: "Meanwhile", "Rich Hours", "The Light Sinks"; *La Traductière*: "My Life without Me", "In a Garden State," "Face Work".

I would also like to thank Joseph Harrison for his acute suggestions, and Michelle de Kretser for all her encouragement.

Contents

Foreword by Mark Strand   11

I

The Mist Lifts	15
Both Hands	16
Megalomania	17
Name Dropping	18
Strange Perfecter	19
Weather Break	20
As Parra Says	21
Meanwhile	22
Far Call	23
Mare's Nest	24
On Earth As It Is	25
Nap	26
A Theory of Next Thursday Night	27
The Same Party	28
Tourism (I)	29
This Way Up	30
The Furry Pages	31
Loose-Pin Hinge	32
Rooms	33
If I Start	34
Log	35
By Accident	36
Re: This Tuesday Morning	37
The Light Sinks	38
Lost and Found	39
Sonic Age	40
Continuous Screening	41
My Life without You	42

II

Sunken Sparkle	45

Contents

The Island and the Capital	47
Dim Thing	50
Burnt Umbrella	52
Summits, Hangars	56
Paradise	57
Late Extra	59
Walking Stick	61

III

Function Centre	71
Rich Hours	72
In a Garden State	73
Pond Life	74
As Le Tellier Says	75
Kitchen in Transit	76
A Different Party	77
A Lead	78
One Thing and Another	79
Face Work	80
Mottoes	81
Zombie Charmers	82
Tourism (II)	83
Invisible Hinges	84
Prop	85
The Penultimate	86
If I Stop	87
Envoy	88

NOTES ON THE TEXT	89
A NOTE ABOUT THE AUTHOR	91
A NOTE ABOUT THE ANTHONY HECHT POETRY PRIZE	93

Foreword by Mark Strand

The first thing that struck me about Chris Andrews' poems was their clarity. No matter how elusive or idiosyncratic the subject the diction was precise. And no matter how plain the world they described or how humdrum the lives they portrayed I felt always the transforming presence of style.

None of this would have been quite so pleasurable if it were not for the calm easily sustained music of the verse and the animating and liberating presence of wit. This is certainly obvious in the way well-known titles and phrases are transformed into humorous sound-alike versions. Hence, we have the neo-Coleridgean "this swamp oil scum my prison," and the austral revision of Psalm 137 "If I forget thee, Wollongong" and even the hedging, if not modest, correction of Neruda, "Tonight I can write if not the saddest lines." This is Andrews at his most playful, but there is a darker aspect to his wit that appears throughout his work. His impressive poem "Burnt Umbrella" begins "It's the end of the beginning of the end" and ends "where it was always the beginning/ of the end of the beginning of something else." Within the downward drift of a young woman's daydreaming are brief, graphic descriptions of a nursing home, a sunset over arid parkland, an unacknowledged call from a telemarketer, all appropriately set in "a world of hit-and-miss proliferation." At one point in this longish, ambitious poem, the young woman gets up from her bed and goes to the window "in time to see a raven inspecting the skeleton of a burnt umbrella." What at first seems just another grim detail becomes suddenly a terrifying image of the angel of death inspecting a skeleton; and the words "in time" instead of being a harmless bit of conversation become resonant with fatality.

Throughout these poems one senses the ghostly presence of the uncanny, moments of implication, and the discontinuous, troubling character of experience. Precision and strangeness play off one another to great effect, as in "Strange Perfecter," a brief dramatization of self-alienation in an already fractured reality. It begins "Who was that strange perfecter occasionally / stepping in to give my life a sideways nudge?" and ends "I was the perfect strang-

Foreword by Mark Strand

er continually / stumbling by chance back into my life to find / it was getting on pretty well without me."

The pressure that time exerts on ourselves no matter what, wearing us and our world down is a constant in Andrews' poetry. The message is dark, as it tends to be in most lyric poetry, but here in Chris Andrews' second book of poems, it is beautifully, memorably articulated.

I

The Mist Lifts

The fickle insolidity of winter
in a higgledy-piggledy city full
of flimsy timber houses and brick veneer
(and stately Victoriana, to be fair)
as opposed to the monumental seasons
of Europe, solemnly inaugurated,
stretching forth like imperial esplanades,
or tropical humidity forever –
that's what we talk about over steaming cups
in low-fat sunlight. It has to be better
than perversely looking forward to the day
when life is finally brought to a standstill
by rigorously transparent procedures.

So this is how the mist lifts in a city
that some gifted children consider the pits
while others at the cutting edge of retro
throw a pinch of wishbone ash into the mix;
it lifts like this off a mirror-still river
where, as it is everywhere, cruelty is
unmistakable as a triangle, but
midwinter's riddled with brilliant days like this.

Both Hands

Dew from the roof is dripping in the down-pipe.
A solitary wisp of cloud evaporates.
On one hand cockatoos are repossessing
the city, on the other, the monsta truck.
Can it be too soon to start making a list
of things you really should get round to doing
(like planning a holiday specially to quench
a passion for promontories and isthmuses)
before you wind up waiting for the charge nurse
to come with her trolley and dole out the pills
or watching your visitors think as they try
to be cheerful, I will be reduced to this?
But they won't know that; they won't even know that,

even if here it can be too late to find
yourself on the receiving end of history.
A beautiful day for it means traffic jams.
Bellbirds are spreading steadily downriver.
On one hand, the mute button, on the other
obligatory necrophiliac close-ups.
Amazing how quiet it looks out the window
as colours and west-facing walls lose their warmth.

Megalomania

The sea my bedside lamp, my endless novel,
my delicate bonfire built of spin drift wood.
The sky my hi-tech oriental factory
seen from a newly built flyover at night.
The night my new dance steps in daft pyjamas,
my Japanese neon bleeding everywhere.
The day my garden of branching cinder paths
their cloud-reflecting puddles lined with ashkeys.
This sun shower screen, this sump oil scum my prism.
This leaf and eyelash mesh my kaleidoscope.
Air your silverish, moon-shot moth ball gown.
The sky my gold dust bath, my busy laundry,
my gradually cooling cup of rose hip tea.

The sea my scrap iron yard, my bitter medicine;
the earth an atoll of lost traffic islands
the day my necklace of lyric instants broke.
That dank air shaft, that snowflake's grave my prison.
The sky my dinted basin, my hearth gone cold.
But ash my seed bed, my poorly hidden key.
Fire my playground cannons facing out to sea.
Fire my grotto full of accidental gold.

Name Dropping

If you're too polite it just confuses things
I thought as I stepped into the gallery.
I don't know what Drew Barrymore was thinking
as she waited to step out (I should admit
I hadn't recognized her, which is funny
because I usually scan strangers' faces,
a habit that makes me a target of choice
for con-men and all sorts of lonesome-eyed strays).
When John came in, after waiting politely,
he told me, and we turned to watch her walking
away in that grainy angelino light
filtered by seaspray and smog (that's John Culbert),
then we went in to look at the collection:

a father was teaching his son to discern
a genetically transmitted nose profile;
I lingered in front of the photo-portraits
taken in plangent, twilit petrol stations.
But dwelling on gaffes can be self-important,
I thought as I stepped out into the evening's
enormous slow performance, and there under
a burgundy hat was Dina Al-Kassim.

Strange Perfecter

Who was that strange perfecter occasionally
stepping in to give my life a sideways nudge?
Or was it just a series of accidents?
Despite the multiplying data there's not
necessarily anyone on your case
in a world where biometric differences
can cover up the gulf that is fixed between
darlings of Morpheus and insomniacs
strapped into the home theatres of their thought,
or between people who feel that the real life
is intimated by bare, windswept uplands
and those who want to live where rhinoplasty
is already as normal as filling teeth.

I was the perfect stranger continually
stumbling by chance back into my life to find
it was getting on pretty well without me
in a world where what people wear correlates
poorly with what they're capable of doing
to someone who'll never be useful to them,
where some can sing an ache to sleep and others
are quite sure they know what intelligence is.

Weather Break

Isolated thunderstorms developing.
Warm enough for you? Geography lessons
recapitulated in the sky: no horst
without its graben, and valleys left hanging
by a mighty glacier that shrank away
under a grey crust of Pleistocene moraine.
When nothing else is happening, weather is.
Meteorologist, how's that for a job?
Out by ten degrees and you don't get the sack.
Me I make one little mistake and the boss ...
Looks like we might be in for some dirty rain.
Chance of a late wash of ripe lemon yellow.
Evanescent wonderforms unravelling.

Bored in the city of happening weather?
For lurid historical postcards, look up:
pleasure domes torched by gawping barbarians
doing their bit to prepare vine-hung ruins
for Enlightened painters to stumble through, filled
with a new kind of wonder, while overhead
snow-laden alps became dusty red mesas.
Whatever's happening, so is the weather.

As Parra Says

Everyone loves to bag the individual
who happens to be inconvenient now
with an ad hoc category: women who make
slow hand gestures to display their burnished nails,
men who walk round with ties over their shoulders …
Maybe not everyone. Speaking for myself,
I hate people who say, "I hate people who …"
As Parra says: I am the individual,
but somewhere in the world my spitting image
goes about his business and, creepier still,
my social doubles write something like this. It's
nice to have things in common, up to a point.
On the other hand, no one likes to be told

"You don't know what it's like," except on TV
where the would-be comforters usually have
more convincing comebacks than, "I'm left-handed,
I can extrapolate …" and the beautiful
suffer in your face. What about what it's like
to seize up when asked, "Where do you see yourself
in five years' time?" Or to have joined the legions
who have stopped smiling because of their bad teeth?

Meanwhile

It was the twenty-first century somewhere
between hay-fever season and leaf meal time.
My father's broken collarbone was knitting.
Defying the pull of our new opiate
(work: since when is it the source of dignity?)
students were using their backs to measure
how long warmth can be stored in a sandstone wall.
Where it was better not to be born, people
were handing over their savings for a way
out of the life trap and onto the death raft.
Where people said, "Wouldn't live anywhere else,"
someone tickled by a dim inkling sat down
and wrote: "It was the seventeenth century ..."

In the capital of our new religion
(desire: it has to be irresistible)
studio millionaire kids were making out
on revolving waterbeds with downtown views
or finding the ice cube root of a gin sling shot
while someone elsewhere maybe wondered how Neil
from *Seven Up* was going and forgot him
within the melting span of a spring hail stone.

Far Call

In a place so advanced all the public phones
are falling forever into disrepair,
black ice coats the pavements. Gingerly, a man
steps through that kingdom of winter and new things:
stair-climbing vacubots, atlases that talk
in anti-rage tones, glossy torrents of hair
pouring in slow motion on flat plasma screens.
Pointy-headed mammals hurry jerkily
past shadow-falls in dim stairwells and foyers.
At last the man finds a public phone that works.
Almost straight away in a far colony
of summer and unreconstructed retro
a mobile plays its tone on a lime green chair

out in the shallows, where schools of blunt-faced fish
are performing smooth simultaneous swerves
over honey-coloured sandstone. Steps away,
a woman turns and stumbles, grasping at air.
Later, battery and sim card lie drying out
beside a slow-cooling cup of ginger tea
while in a sky deepening to ultramarine
a plover calls a plover calls a plover.

Mare's Nest

A nightmare can drag you back to the whirlpool
churning plastic bags in a dingy thicket
but rearing office blocks may also recall
a rock jumble rising into a bright haze,
the way up marked by subtle rearrangements:
how many stones does it take to make a cairn?
You can lead a dark horse to still waters but
beware the hefty anger of the placid,
the elephantine anger of the placid:
go tell the dust to hurry up and settle.
An empty hill seen from the freeway may ring
a dream bell, but if there isn't an exit
you have to drive on through a bitumen world.

A well full of weeds can keep a secret but
what do you make a container from to hold
the universal solvent: cynic acid?
A lighthouse no longer identified by
the length of the dark lapse between its flashes
will do you a coffee. Painted waymarks fade
but an old dog can still teach you how to stretch
and a blind mare can show you to the ocean.

On Earth As It Is

It takes the strong-handed and the mixed-handed;
some people paralyzed by hesitation
and regret getting pushed aside by others
who have never been wrong in their lives. It takes
shiners-in-a-crisis and long-haul copers;
the briskly and in a way thoughtlessly kind
and those who find comfort in distributing
blame or inventing computer viruses.
It takes just a few real monsters and heroes
but plenty of people naturally enough
supposing that the obvious differences
are the causes of the less obvious ones,
to make this world anyway, such as it is,

with its actors in Mogadishu dubbing
Bollywood romances into Somali,
its prophets of serendipitous reuse,
and its bush mechanics packing spinifex
into flat tires; our world with its worm farm hands,
its war widowers filling watering cans
and its philosophers pondering whether
there is something it is like to be a ghost.

Nap

A ten-minute Jesuit nap with shoes on
releases the hypnagogic sentences
mimicking the rhythms of sports commentary,
morphing darkly into a story like this:
In the sunless world where we'd arranged to meet
everything's lit from within and space has nerves
that pass through your throat (if you slide along them
like a curtain ring it will hurt the next day)
but it turned out to be much harder to leave
my body behind than my slugabed mind,
so we plumped for the Donkey on Fire instead
with its comforting smell of public carpet,
billiard balls clacking and vinyl silences.

Having lit my way through the gloom with a pint,
I slumped on a couch to watch elastic blobs
collide and coalesce in a lava lamp.
How is it possible to return from there
with the briefly glowing certitude that all
is forgiven and a hypnopompic snap
of softly obliterated prints left by
a barefoot Carmelite errand in the snow?

A Theory of Next Thursday Night

Of the following we can be fairly sure:
a parma and pot deal at the corner pub,
drunken stragglers cursing as they bruise their shins
on muscle-building contraptions (it will be
hard rubbish collection eve), night stencilers
scattering their situationist faces
with is it a serious smile on their lips?
Indecision browsing through new releases:
indy pap or action heroes to show us
how real men take more than an eye for an eye.
The moon will be nearly full; someone is bound
to see a bat fly in front of it. Given
four billion streams of human experience

(say the rest of us are dreamlessly asleep)
calendar clichés and judicial errors
will happen, daydreams and nightmares will come true
somewhere. Someone may quit pitching her idea
for a film and start writing a book instead.
An adolescent butterfly collector
woken by a new catch dimly fluttering
in the showcase might come to a decision.

The Same Party

You missed the *best* night it was *so* fantastic.
It was travel bore meet renovation bore.
Someone threw up into a grand piano.
Renovation, sort of, more making the lounge
a cabinet of minimalist wonders
with fresh inward windows and Conundrum rugs.
It was just a baby and a *baby* grand.
She'd travelled to places I'd barely heard of:
countries in Africa, suburbs in Melbourne.
She'd been to the dead heart of car world on foot.
The pianist transposed it up an octave.
Axiological differences were aired:
That is *such* a bad song. But as someone said:

"Boredom is the dream bird that hatches the egg
of experience," and the boringest bore
of all is bored bore. Excitement was mounting
as if towards ecstatic catalysis
and then it was subsiding like nausea.
The widow from next door called with secateurs.
Our host in the laundry filling a bucket
said: "Not much point trying to own your big day."

Tourism (I)

Cumulus clouds are surprisingly sharp-edged
even seen close up from a plane as its wing
goes plunging into one. And it's sobering
how even a big city seen from the air
at night is an atoll in a black ocean.
Or maybe that's just atavistic worry
about arriving somewhere unfamiliar
after dark. Say it's Melbourne. You're curious
to see how the wretched in-flight video
will map onto ground-level reality
when you walk the vaunted malls and recognize
ingeniously designed public spaces
used by citizens to shoot up and die in.

It's hard to adjust to the length of the days
and the washing machine cycles, but your guide
from Ordinary Life Tours will understand.
When you've seen smog-defying monster elms,
or sumo wrestling in fat suits at the pub,
and the Southern Kite, you can lie down and fail
to get your head around how it all might be
a multiverse made from dancing bits of string.

This Way Up

I can walk backwards but it makes my neck hurt.
When I was a kid the right knee of my pants
usually tore first, but I can only sneer
on the left. In a gravitational field,
my body goes this way up for sixteen hours
then should be laid flat in the dark. If I said
it wasn't ticklish, how obvious was that?
Prick and it'll bleed, so careful with that Ouch!
Failing a lotus with a puff of ether
in it at the centre of this opaque space,
small sorts of flora and fauna multiply:
it's the tropical, Hindu sort of temple.
The sight of a workstation makes my back hurt.

Some bodies are happy sitting at the still
centre of a drive-thru tarscape. Not this one.
Sometimes after a sunny lunch I forget
the whole universe doesn't have to take arms
to knock it flat. A drop of liquid will do.
Pretty good the way it keeps bouncing back though,
so far, slower than it did at first, but still.
Neutrinos flood through it like wind through a ghost.

The Furry Pages

It's no help to say, If it wasn't taken
for granted it wouldn't really be coping,
or to point out that etymologically
euphoric means good at bearing things; it won't
stop a rash of tiny giving-up events
proliferating in the brain, to the point
where tidying seems unbearably complex.
Even sound advice can smell like the furry
dental-yellow pages of a self-help book
in an op-shop when winter strips the world back
to its true colours – grey and gray – or summer
shows its underface, cicada shells for eyes,
the orange sun rising like a death ray lamp.

You know chances are this too will pass away
but if it was only a matter of time
I suppose you wouldn't really be hoping
that a day will come when what you have to do
will feel as simple as clearing disused lanes
of spiderwebs sagging with dew, following
faint waymarks from a bridge to a weed-choked well
and resting there on cloth- and flesh-worn coping.

Loose-Pin Hinge

While someone has to look through the detective's
Book of Offenders, nobody has to be
mounting an expedition to liberate
the city of which the lord mayor is a child
surrounded by lycanthropic sycophants.
Nobody has to be counting butterflies
of breath, or distilling the brightness that falls
from the air down to a brimming thimbleful.
As long as the antelope's strategy works
for humans, it is incumbent on no one
to hang a doll's house door on a loose-pin hinge,
or Chinese lanterns in a peep-box model
of earth as it might be, somewhere, for a while.

Somebody has to be Postmaster General
but no one has to be reconstituting
a dream of "peach-blown" darkness falling over
an ashen shore where all the lost were massing.
There are so many things that nobody must
be doing, and some are being done. Without
the unnecessary something would be missing
but it wouldn't necessarily be missed.

Rooms

A hospital room not yet claimed from the sky
somewhere over a weather-swept cityscape,
a volume not even modelled in 3D
as yet, with its transient contents of rain,
starlings, knobbly pollen, the odd plastic bag
hanging puffed up where a last breath will be held
and released. Or is this faceless cubicle
that wires and pipes will climb to a container
for the silent rejoicing of a student
who, on his first night there, will watch the slow stretch
of moonlight lozenges, wondering why he's come
so far south in the world, beginning to feel
all-swallowing emptiness open inside?

Now men in toxic green who guard the hard-won
belief that it's undignified to hurry
backhoe through generations of ash, perhaps,
and in a new secure apartment complex
a child relieved to have some time on her hands
feels the smoother band along a bluestone wall
where prisoners each locked in an intimate cage
of lice would jostle for a place in the sun.

If I Start

I remember telling my future self, Don't
start thinking these were the best days of your life
or I'll disown you. I remember the wind,
still chilly but not unkind, stripping blossom
out of a rain-laden plum tree and bustling
the back end of an apricot storm away
while citrus sidelight put a fugitive glow
into bricks and tiles and gave wet bitumen
sparkling relief. I was going to covet
records, some of which I squirm to remember.
On the cover of one I never owned were
four differently-coloured balloons in a row
resting on a sky-filled mirror of wet sand.

I think I remember that musical spring
of pure possibilities. The problem is,
there's documentary evidence to prove
that my past self was morosely nostalgic
already: If I forget thee, Wollongong ...
Why should I care about being disowned by *him*?
I don't. But may I bite my tongue if I start
running down the worthwhile things I haven't done.

Log

Frosty conditions and early fog then fine.
A hot air balloon in the shape of a house.
A manhole cover rocking when it's stepped on.
A sour-smelling pair of trousers in the tram.
The silk of the lyric stretched over the frame
of the melody, up it soars like a kite,
except that it's one of those lyrics that goes,
Babe, you're too good for me (bring on the next one).
More than a hint of Obsession in the lift.
The grin of a girl who's learnt not to relax.
A cold waterfall stripped away by the wind.
A gradually deflated jumping castle.
Fine apart from isolated thunderstorms.

A hailstone the size of a six-year-old fist.
A rat's tail flopping against struts in the wall.
The orange anchorman smiles: good news at last,
except that it's one of those stories about
a miracle cure, maybe, one day, too late
for anyone with the disease watching now.
A ship in a bottle afloat on the sea.
Insinuations of sleepless foliage.

By Accident

Tonight I can write if not the saddest lines,
the sort that drive a resonant ache in deep
like the shockingly slow cover of "Fast Car"
I heard as I lay in a black hotel room
feeling fine, then lines that gather drabber kinds
of sadness, like knowing which were the best days:
sad like a stand-up routine that's not working,
or the dated cover art on videos;
sad by accident like the fall of a song
from edgy to catchy to muzak classic,
or was that a fatality like fresh clerks
finding out the translucent brutalities
and slender consolations of office life?

Tonight I can write for example: the stars
are shot-holes in the roof of a ghost town hall,
and schoolie debris is strewn on cold beach sand:
the vomit of losers, a solitary thong,
sad like someone who has heard by accident
a snatch of what people say behind his back
without a trace of anger in their voices,
and thought: I probably say that sort of thing.

Re: This Tuesday Morning

Steam is flowing upwards from our drinks. The sky
our brindled dairy cow lumbering along.
Wattle birds plunge out of pollen-dusted shade
into a shivering volume of sunlight.
We're wondering just how anatomical
the difference is between male and female gaits,
and who said the first time is always the last
first time too. But it's better than complaining
about how the institution has assumed
the fragile egotist's craving for esteem,
or morbidly anticipating the day
when actions are definitively frozen
by the reasonable fear of litigation.

So this is how we thrash out the list of things
to be done before eating and excreting
get messy again. Here comes the cloud shadow.
A scab dries. A drip taps. A root lifts the tar.
Blackbird song fills out a gap in the traffic.
In spite of everything, the high heel survives.
And a girl walks by saying, He had the best
smile ever though don't you reckon on a boy?

The Light Sinks

It's day number sixteen thousand and something
and what have I seen? A dense flock of finches
performing a sharp simultaneous turn,
a litmus strip of sky, low sunlight slipping
gold coins into the mouth of a laughing man,
fake wood fires really flaming in a shop front,
pink sweaters in a hot gym, the robber's cave
of night sliding slowly open, the marvels
of light bouncing around all over the place
or almost: my visual field is punctured
by the pupils of other people, like wells
in a landscape or loopholes in a stronghold,
staring deep into which will tell me nothing,

though much can be inferred from blinks and twitches
of corrugator and depressor muscles,
more or less insightfully, for simple tests
suggest that this too is unfairly shared out:
skill at reading states of mind from strips of face,
which could be useful, marginally, maybe,
if ever you're counting the days in a place
where guards look in through a slot, then slide it shut.

Lost and Found

Think. There are only so many places. Think.
In regrowth scrub you could be just feet away,
but is it better to see for empty miles?
During the last world war a British sailor
survived for four and half months on a raft
after his ship was sunk off the Azores.
It's true such cases are rare, but they exist.
Check the records at the Bureau Veritas.
Lost: leader, fiftyish, good at not blinking,
has undergone bewildering conversion.
Found: poetry pieces, almost complete set,
assembly instructions poorly translated.
It's not a question of holding out much hope –

you just don't know, like they told us at the pound.
One day about ten years ago a young man
set out to climb a volcano in Chile.
His parents in Holland would still like to hear
from anyone who might identify him
by the brand of his watch or his running shoes.
But there are so many places they could be.
It's not a question of holding out much hope.

Sonic Age

Sounds that came into the world in my lifetime
already sound old-fangled: dial-up modems,
the implosion of a television tube
in a set dropped from a high window. Green geeks
go digitally capturing lyre-bird gronks
and atavistically soothing aggregates
of infinitesimal sonic events
like pine needles rubbing in ruddy darkness
or droplets falling back into the ocean.
Grist to the mill of the marvellous creatures
firm in their briefly shared belief that music
is all around us, even in chords hammered
on a Wurlitzer electric piano

or commuters chatting (the vernacular
turns up fully new (not) intensifiers),
though many are now absorbed in pocketfuls
of sound: a satin voice whispering "Enter
the silence," a robot singing E MO TION
with touching persistence. Everyone can feel
the rails joining under the wheels of the train,
while deaf kids sign and double up with laughter.

Continuous Screening

Hanging out the washing makes me watch the sky.
Slow pan over cinematographic cloud:
crumbling frescoes and collapsing parapets.
A background for near-enough-to-matching socks,
a T-shirt explicably fallen from grace,
faded to sky-blue pink and pegs weathered grey.
It may not be much of a drying day but
this is the sky I was born to live under:
split-level interiors intimating
the ghost-life that never seems to age (perhaps
because it's imaginary, which might mean
mine to assemble in imagination
from parts never meant to compose any whole

yet), full of activity, promising rain
to make me remember the shape of the roof,
to stipple beaches and percolate until
there can't be a dry corner left in the soil,
indiscriminate rain that falls all over
wedding plans and military operations
branded for cable news, precision hairdos
and the rubble of what was whole this morning.

My Life without You

I've glimpsed what it might have been like on my trips
to places that weren't even disappointing,
just real and so almost utterly foreign
to flimsy, film-set imaginings. The real
with its detail filled in far beyond the call
of duty set up peephole installations:
a kind man's flat into which nothing useless
and beautiful had been brought for a long time;
a window display of high-heeled work boots; keys
but not mine, a pink sapphire ring and false teeth
in a lost-property box; something half-dead
floating in the eyes of a man who turned out
to be not only a cold fish but a shark.

Next year it will be twenty years already.
You've probably forgotten most of the times
you made all the difference (if you ever knew)
by not being otherwise than as you are:
a perfect stranger to dinginess. You were
the barefoot breeze all along the branching path,
the breathable light and the ocean-washed air.
It was you. I knew it. I had no idea.

II

Sunken Sparkle

The luminous youth of a relative's car
(there were three in the drive)
made her think as she squeezed past of mica,
flakes of it spinning in a river,
(that sunken sparkle) and snow

imagined in slow motion
after American films and before
a future afternoon when she
would see it for real from the window
of an empty flat grown dim behind her.

A rose thorn caught her shirt.
Stopping to disentangle it
under the kitchen window she heard:
"No, it's always fifty metres
from wherever you are. There's no place
he can touch you."
                    Legally, she thought,
stepping into the sun-pummelled street.

It must have been her aunt's new car.
Giulia, with her gross lipstick
– "Roach" by Urban Decay –
and the spooky exactitude of her gifts.
It must have been her ringing round last night.

Cutting behind the bowling club
she felt a spider's anchor-line stretch
and almost imperceptibly snap
against her lip. A rustle in the palm
and a honk made her look up
into the blood-red wing-pit of an ibis.

Sunken Sparkle

She didn't notice an overturned cockroach,
still alive but already crawling
with ants or a concave pink addition
to the chewing-gum archive.

She was thinking of the holidays,
the second-last school holidays
stretching ahead of her emptily
and the dark back of a drawer
where preparations for the voyage
to the Kingdom of winter and old things
had begun with a box of slides
salvaged from the purge,
miniatures by which to remember
lives grown dim behind her one day,
including an Apollonian torso
with plastic cricket bat
glowing on an early evening beach,
headless but identifiable
by the relative youth of a luminous scar.

The Island and the Capital

A woman ironing. A stain
faint in the smooth wake of the iron.
She stops. Looks out the window. Sees
far over the ranges of tiles
a side-lit chimney somehow like
that small bare island in the lake
near home she never set foot on.

The iron cooling on its heel,
the blue cloth smooth over the table,
she stops to examine a spoon, sits down,
and, as along the verge of sleep,
catches herself imagining,
the Capital,
               the capital.

Not as it was when, last of all,
she heaved her trunk off the country bus:
Saturday night, it was raining.

Looking for a place out of the crush
too frightened to go into a café
switching the trunk from hand to hand
pursued by a lottery-ticket vendor
retracing her steps as if compelled
bruising her knee against the trunk
too tired to decide which café now
just looking for a place out of the rain.

Finally she found a square,
a free bench under its one tree,
straightened out her fingers, unfolded
the map drawn by the priest at home
to show her the way to the convent
where she went apprehensive under arches

The Island and the Capital

to the refectory with its heavy spoons
and the dormitory its thick sheets.

Not like that, but as it was
when she was early for the airport bus:
Sunday morning, clear.

Before the darkness was a crack ajar
both her eyes had opened wide at once.
The iron-bound gates swung shut behind her,
and before she got to the end of the street
the lamps inside the trees went out.
At the terminus with an hour to spare
she exchanged her trunk for the number 1
and she was off, her body light
and full of sleep and wide awake,

the crowds gone deeper into the city,
the mist blown away, the net of water
over the stones broken beyond repair.

To the great square all hers
except for the Presidential guards
silent under their brilliant helmets
distorting the deserted balconies,
and still as the bodies of cold water
asleep in the marble basins.

Led by a liquid sound up a stepped street,
she took a handful of water from a lion's mouth.
And when a woman leant from a high window
to tell her it was a dead end,
she turned as if she had already known,
turned again and there it was:

The Island and the Capital

the Sanctuary,
               the sanctuary
built with the saint's own delicate hands,
duller than the picture in the classroom.

First into the airport bus
she pressed the wad of papers in her pocket,
unworried by the thought of never coming back.

A man on his way home home, somewhere.
He is late. Cars rarer now.
It starts to rain. She thinks of the skids
beyond her hearing, lengthening.
At the front door a probing key
and fumbling through the bunch. She stops
wiping a bent spoon. Gets up.

It must have been next door.

Dim Thing

Just a moment midnight
never promised anything.
It's not the slender centre-pole
of a cobalt-blue marquee
astray among the crescent dunes
or anything.

It's more like exorbitant corkage
or estuarine indecision or
smoke of damp particle-board.

Midnight is discontinuous
nowhere between the chimes out of sync,
in none of the wobbly time zones so
stop thinking of it as a front
sweeping the dark side of the earth
like the luminous foam of the swash
that seethes away, all away,
or even a chain of hilltop bonfires:
embers, cinders, ashes, dust.

Lozenges of moonlight maybe
stretching over the bathroom lino
and the tickle of residual addiction.

Midnight is a dim thing really
not a purifying deflagration
in the mind's eye of a copycat arsonist.
I don't mean concealed like an envelope
warm in a silk-lined tuxedo pocket,
or an ant-lion snug in its sunken parlour.
It has absolutely nothing to do
with the great greasy hinge-pin upon which
or anything pivotal at all.

Dim Thing

Silence after sirens more like it
or guttural haruspication or
a cat in a cooling undercarriage.

Before you can say there it's over.
Tomorrow already but the night still callow.
The tram tracks stop dead just like that,
but a crosswind goes on stripping
the empty beaches of the sky.

Burnt Umbrella

It's the end of the beginning of the end,
she thought. From here on in doors close. September:
pittosporum hedges releasing their scent,
fresh elm-shade thickening, a light pollen breeze.
The Parade stretching off to the north, where the gold was.
Students with their art of straggling,
each a sovereign over wild acres of time.
Wait till you get to the office, she thought.

She honestly saw a failure factory
in the place of a conservatorium.
Run by failures. One stepped out.
You have your captive audience now,
but wait till you hit retirement, she thought.
She couldn't stop calculating the sum,
the imaginary sum of all sad things.

The nursing home: roses thriving on drought.
A woman smoking in a wheelchair
outside the unopening automatic doors,
laughing with the immigrant aides
at some sundowner losing it again.

She thought of mothers far away
with no one to help them turn over in bed,
an uncle with emphysema soon too weak
to sit up straight and lift his food,
and men being scolded in hospitals
for not looking after themselves.
But are they, she wondered, so wrong
not to have ended up here?

The Avenue veered away to the west
beside a low dome of scorched parkland.
Joggers came thumping and huffing along,

Burnt Umbrella

men who sold their time in six-minute units.
One gave her a free spot valuation
of her desirability: fair
to moderate, at a distance, still. And his?
But she didn't care about his.

At home she went straight to the bedroom, lay down
and stared at the water-damaged ceiling rose,
thinking, Soon it will already be too late,
almost relieved as if it already was.
The window gave onto a lane:
gritty blows of small, hard heels,
the indolent slap and drag of thongs,
jasmine patiently wrecking a fence,
with its scent of years ago and next weekend.

She curled up tightly on the bed
as if she wanted to withdraw through herself,
grow backwards, shedding errors and stains,
back into the womb to be deconceived.
It's the surest way to stop thinking about it,
she thought. It's not the future.
I just want the present to stop.

Books on the bedside table. One began:
"The brain is a work and we don't know it,"
but she hadn't been able to read for weeks.
Her life was objectively going pretty well.
And she knew that, as much as she could.
She was twenty-nine, employed, single-ish,
free of life-threatening illnesses still,
and never quite good enough
at anything, in any way, she thought.

Burnt Umbrella

Voices from the lane: "... she's not Australian ...
so you don't get all that temperamental stuff ..."
She swung her feet to the floor and sat up
in time to see a raven inspecting
the skeleton of a burnt umbrella.
But there was still a falling in her,
a wanting to be ill or just a habit
of gathering evidence to prove
that life as it is in itself is atrocious.

The telephone rang. Someone far away
said, "I am not trying to sell you anything ..."
She laid the receiver gently on the table
and as she heard that tiny voice go on

remembered her own brief experience
as a door-to-door hawker of large bad pictures:
the cynical training seminar,
the far-flung target suburbs
with their treeless bending streets and dead-end places,
the painting she sold, a tinny glint on the water,
a patch of deep Naples yellow in the sunset sky
like a precious oriental miniature,
milk billowing in her tea, the Marie biscuit
she selected from an ample assortment,
the couple's protective curiosity,
the fussy perfection of their maritime bathroom,
how little the sale had depended on art,

but most of all she remembered the sense
of the world wrapped around her as she waited
to be picked up on a high corner: the sky
Baltic blue over an ocean of tiles,
a world of hit-and-miss proliferation

Burnt Umbrella

– bathroom fittings and biscuit concepts,
toxic sweat-shops and artist-run spaces –

opening out and falling away,
shedding pods and husks and chrysalids,
naturally gathering scars and stains,
a world of wet casements and hinges working loose,
where it was always the beginning
of the end of the beginning of something else.

Summits, Hangars

A smooth cavity of flesh-worn stone
loses the warmth of the day's last hand.
In a side chapel, canvases loom
dim with candle soot. A warden stands
by the church door holding a long key.
Christmas lights are about to go live
in plane trees. A rough outgrowth of bone
wears cartilage in an arthritic knee.
Eyes lock onto a solitary tart
going stale and salivary glands
spurt. A guide from a faraway part
of the former empire shows how gold
falling from the sky left painters free
to chisel new summits of bright cold
and scoop out backless hangars of gloom.
Eyes made slow by the ages of art
trace the profile of a guard for whom
the museum is everyday life
seriously smiling at his phone
beside a window subtly alive
with a cloistered chestnut tree's dim gold.

Paradise

The rigid space of midday is a prison
for citizens of the universe by night
excitably declaring, We invented
the real – we can begin again like Adam
rejoining the dots so people will look up
and see the safety pin or the cicada
prickle the blue expanse of finishing dusk.
Our new geometry sets can trace the line
that runs between knowing you'll never know much
and being proud of not knowing certain things,
between what might take generations to turn
around and what is as irresistible
as time flowing in the middle of the night.

But even the grand utopians belong
to the line of red Adam; eventually
they fold their differences back into the dark
and sleep, while a sight awaits the itchy eyes
of east-coast insomniacs anonymous:
between the leaden gray of the breathless sea
and the blank-slate grey of the shelterless sky
a stroke of light irreversibly affirmed
like the red outline of beginning Adam.

Between the wine glass bay and the dusk-charged air
between the earth worm cast and the fire fly trap
the rudder pin shears the wind break water falls
between the drift wood fire and the wish bone ash
between the sea lane change and the sky light house.

The green sweep of evacuated Eden
glimpsed in a rear-view mirror. Darkness falling
like a blow for the shelterless far from home
between a top-heavy sky and the ocean
without footholds, invisibly divided

Paradise

by a border sleepless eyes invigilate.
Somewhere round here the West or the North begins.
Paradise from the Persian for "walled around".
This is where we have to draw the line because.
There's an opening in the razor wire game
for a flexible supplier to corrections.

Late Extra

A trace of the wine of the shy
still adrift in his blood
but all the bitterness slept off.
Damp in his pockets
and a high wind in the hair
of someone with a life all of her own
who pored over a window box
half way to the land of chimneys
as he dodged the mustardy dogshit scuffed
down the street of the fallen young here.

No watch, no map, no overcoat.
A couple of words under his breath.
Bearings snatched from the look of a street,
the way it turns or falls away,
its unfamiliarity,
the litmus strip of sky.

A matter of never stretching the pace
or cutting it short behind. And patience
because it takes a long time
to walk your momentum into the pavement
so you become a weightless register:

a cloth bag
full of the wind of your own motion;
the colours of a raw wall
quilted on the gutter stream
going down the pupil's plughole;
a footstep's echo in the arch of a bridge
punctuating, deep in the inner ear,
traces of a listening yesterday.

But the gate of the winter garden slammed
behind him, sending a shiver

Late Extra

into every gilded spearhead on the fence.
And he saw the last thread of snow come apart,
melting into turned earth,
a wet flag wrapped around the pole,
and dilute sunlight sink into a marble ear,
lifelike in translucency.

Defatiguable after all and still
he had to split the crush
of people who get in the way
and look at you,
whose cheek skin shakes
about fixed lips
at each stiff tread.

Eyes on the ground he tried to see
an asymmetry of eyelids
the diameter of the earth away.

The scenery swarming with late extras.
One more come to number old stones
in the city of bells out of phase,
of bishops riding high in the mist,
the city black with footprints,
green with rust.

From a bridge, between day and night,
he could stare into the vaulted river
that is still a river,
boiling where the steps go under,
spinning in the wake of a stranded lamp-post;
the cutwaters turning it over
and the blunt prow of a barge
labouring upstream,
just fitting under the arch.

Walking Stick

The receiver was still lying on the table.
She picked it up: not the volumetric silence
of the stalking calls she perfected her technique on,
but pure disconnection, dead wire, beautiful.

In Hyderabad or wherever it was,
the project manager had probably set
a "kill-time" for non-responding customers
like her, known in the trade as "ghosts" or "holes".

Morning still at the call-centre there
with its multilingual background chat and snacks
bought before sunrise at street stalls lit
with expertly pirated electricity.

Evening already here between brown parks.
Daylight saved for planting succulents
and living the dream of the deck: a clean outdoors.
She set the receiver gently back in its cradle.
Turtle-dove dialogue. Flooded lawn-mower.
Late in the day for nail-gun shots.
A faint scent of forgotten toast.

Shallow diagonals of light showed up the dust
on the window ledge and her slewed CDs.
The Mysterious Barricades. And The Planks.
It wasn't their fault she had listened to them
far too much at one time in her life.
She opened the jewel case, took out the disc,
as if it had the sharp and unclean edges
of a tin can lid, and put it on to play.
But it wasn't the soundtrack of a drift
towards disaster, strewn with clues.
It wasn't about her, it wasn't about, it was
a phantom palace built from dreck:

Walking Stick

patiently aged and damaged sounds,
acid-bathed chords almost falling apart,
childlike keyboard melodies distressed
by long exposure to the west-coast sun,
forever mysterious party chat
from a cassette discovered by accident,
friction of callused fingertips
on wire-wound strings, electro-peeps
and documentary birdsong captured
at the very beginning of Spring.

Like a luminous 3-D blueprint traced
in her darkening flat, it was architecture,
building, opening, filling itself in,
billowing, swelling, pulling itself free
of all her associations (the way
she kept thinking at every step, *I knew
this would happen, I knew it.*
And the waiting, the poison, the soul rot).

It was "the soundtrack of the alternative place
you might be right now," except
the place was just a metaphor for what
was happening there in her flat, in her:
invisible but as real as anything
you might stub your toe on in the dark,
and driven by an inner necessity
the world had done without until when?

She looked for a date on the case
but the yellow-blue light of the sky
was too dim by then to read print that fine.

Walking Stick

The shadow-line was climbing
the jasmine-smothered fence outside
and the burnt umbrella's skeleton was gone.

A squeeze-torch lay on the window-ledge,
packed with visible plastic cogs and wire.
They were giving them away at The Light in Winter,
where she had heard an American say:
So this is a torch? and imagined him
imagining a flaming tallow-sodden rag
defying the empire of night.
(Later, jammed in a crowd,
she was groped by a smiling creep.)

There was still juice in the battery.
"Recorded at Hexagon Sun," the fine print said,
"2002." She turned. The bluish beam
swung over the spines of her books
and came to rest on a postcard collage
entitled "The Undiscovered Country"
showing a rugged-up rambler surveying
the valley of Great Langdale, Cumbria,
its baize floor invaded by shadow,
a silver star on a far mountainside
marking the spot where discovery might lead
or begin. In the lower right-hand corner,
an ad for Dr Williams' Pink Pills:
"The Simplest Beauty Treatment in the World":
for "Glowing Health, Clear Skin,
Colourful Cheeks and Lips,"
but also, in that barefaced age,
"a vitalizing tonic for the not so young."

Walking Stick

Beside the card was a plastic box of slides
labelled DUDS & DOUBLES. She held one up
but all she could make out against
the orange of the countertwilight
was an indeterminate curly-haired silhouette,
so she took the box and torch into the kitchen
and projected the image onto the fridge.
It was her at age – what? – 17?
Glowing health, colourful cheeks and lips.

The next one was a total blur:
jellyfish folds of Aurora Australis?
Then, against a background of populated surf,
a torso cut off at shoulder level,
but she could recognize it as her father's
by the luminous relative youth of a scar.
Then a field through a breach in a wall,
strewn with butter-coloured rolls of hay.
(All of this before the present
was eaten by a reconstructed past.)

Her prints were on the torch and everywhere.
The flat was full of evidence
of what she had done in almost thirty years,
most of them spent in this city, "the hole",
as she had sometimes called it, but also
"the only place I'm really sure exists."
Reticulate city with millions of switches
flipping and its eastern edge
already gone into the dark.

A fire could destroy the flat
but there would still be traces left outside,
and nothing she could do would ever alter that,

Walking Stick

(not even the simplest beauty treatment:
pure disconnection, an end to the present).

What she hadn't done, more like,
but all the evidence could only
ever serve to reconstruct
a skeleton agenda,
and every piece of it was also
something in itself: the torch,
the postcard and the shelf it rested on,
built in her grandfather's garage
where butter-coloured curls of wood
fell from the plane onto oily cement:
a night underfoot with its stardrops of solder.

Even the little celluloid squares
staring off into the past
at the glories of seventies hair or dogs
asleep on a railway platform south of Naples,
those records of the lost and gone
or changed were present there and then
and changing: mould was darkening desert skies,
colour was leaching from cheeks and lips
and not even scanning would make them immortal.

Duds, doubles, discards, rejects:
scenes from the continuous life of light,
filtered, reflected, refracted, absorbed,
descending a light well exhausted to touch
the perished, dusty rubber of a dummy
and full-colour catalogues drenched and crisped,
shining off a smooth new scar,
glowing bottle-green through a wave
as it rears, groomed by an onshore breeze,
coming to rest inside a grape.

Walking Stick

She switched off the torch and squeezed it,
felt its mechanism purring in her hand,
then laid it gently on the table.
The television screen seemed to be glowing.
The window was an oblong of deepening purple
with wing lights stitching across the top.
Even the way she knew that everything
was changing irreversibly was changing
and the past had no bottom to get to in the end.

Light spilled from the opening fridge.
She poured a glass of tonic water,
listened to it seething and imagined
bubble shadows streaming up the walls
but the burnt smell was disturbingly strong.

She went out onto the balcony. The door
of her neighbour's flat was wide open.
A layer of toast smoke floated at head-level.
He was coughing and struggling with the sash
of his kitchen window, a wispy-haired silhouette
against the paler grey of the light well.

It was the first time she had seen inside
the mirror-image of the space she lived in.
It seemed to be bristling with parlour palms.
A cat walked slowly up the runner towards her.

She turned and leaned on the iron railing,
looking over the low dome of scorched parkland.
The lights of the children's hospital winked
through a curtain of gum leaves combing the breeze.

Walking Stick

A manhole cover rocked under someone's foot.
A raven cawed with a strange upward inflexion.
Rails joined under the wheels of a distant tram.
The adjustable joint in a walking stick clicked.

III

Function Centre

Resonant surgical anecdotes roll on:
spiral fractures from middle-aged skateboarding.
Old antipathies are instantly renewed:
"Still writing away for X-Ray Spex, I see!"
When it comes to stories of jumping the fence
– "It was like I'd been walking insincerely" –
many think I told you so, some feel cheated.
Vanity comes creeping out through tiny cracks
to bask in the sun: It was so cold in there!
But what's-her-name still speaks just often enough
for her silence not to be significant.
Outside: fractured slabs of concrete glistening.
Frangipani flowers lie crushed in the round.

Departing steps have a pasty sibilance.
A pair of near-perfect strangers, one patting
pockets in search of a lighter, the other
returning to return a mistaken coat,
make the first moves of what could turn out to be
a long conversation begun at the end
of a reunion where late-bloomers gloated
over the popular blonde who peaked too soon.

Rich Hours

Every mind has its weather, predictable
only up to a point: electricity
strikes out of the blue and the wind shifts like this,
imperceptibly, so later you can't say
when or guess why it might have begun to blow
from that unlikely region always beyond
the horizon, bringing a scent of cut hay
safely stored. But before I or my doubles
could even think it might be worth writing this,
others were throwing sticks to knock down acorns
for pigs, gathering in the sheaves before it rained,
or crushing lapis lazuli to make paint
of a novel shade known as overseas blue

without a thought for their image on the web,
or which sub-generation they belonged to,
rarely supposing that their lives might be worth
more than three lines in a parish register,
just hoping they'd still be around in five years,
though curious perhaps in their not-so-rich hours
about fashion or boredom, or even moods
that others had better take into account.

In a Garden State

Glow-in-the-dusk lemons ripen in the sun,
slow-flung grape-vine tendrils grapple spirally,
scrambled-egg roses smother a leaning shed
while a speckled fledgling sporting woefully
inadequate tail feathers bumbles under
the sleepy gaze of a veteran predator
and ribbons of birdsong tangle in the breeze.
All the abyssal variety of life
seeming to get it right just like that, wearing
its billions of years of mistakes so lightly.
This too can be found in nature: H E L P Y O U R S E L F
chalked beside a veteran lime green chair bearing
a box of lemons, yet when you remember

ideologues, bureaucrats and psychopaths
in atrociously stable symbiosis,
or the naturalist's take on *Schadenfreude*
(there's nothing deep or personal about it:
it's simply that things going badly for you
means they might be that bit easier for me),
it's not all that hard to get your head around
how something can be both natural and wrong.

Pond Life

Bored by ancestral love-letters once posted
in a gap in a wall where the wind still moans,
I was transparent but only to others,
like my third cousin's anatomical doll.
I sensed he was tactfully not exploiting
the unfair advantage of experience,
while spying things in me that I was dimly
unaware of, as a student of pond life
with a mind full of field-guide illustrations
might spy, beneath rafts of caddis-fly cases
made of anything a silken thread can bind,
a stirring in the murk, not that he was prone
to creeping monster-hero moralism

– as if only heroes could make a difference,
as if every foible were symptomatic
of a cunningly concealed monstrosity.
His passion was the young science of genetics
which would soon, he claimed, be able to explain
the passing on of a truly frightening sneeze
or a smile realized by remote forbears
with teeth worn down by sand from a windmill stone.

As Le Tellier Says

I came away from that seminar thinking
Losers would have to be better company.
A headache was having itself in my head.
The city was glowing like an ember-cave,
but the wind smelt like snow. As Le Tellier says,
The day you begin to believe you deserve
your good luck, that's when you become an arsehole.
Only the magic of fear had been holding
me down in my seat. I could get up and walk
away from that rigorous river of grey
flowing on behind me, professionally.
Happily the city was riddled with bars
competing for the title of best hidden.

I'd rather be doing brute mood improvement.
I'd rather be astray in a dictionary
– ember week: a week in which ember days fall –
or taking a gap for a walk in the hope
of stumbling on the missing piece by a stroke
of crackpot luck, never mind how fat the chance.
Go figure the proportion of ice crystals
with three- not six-fold symmetry in the sky.

Kitchen in Transit

My mother was knitting up a ravelled sleeve.
Everyone else in the flat was fast asleep
like dinghies in a creak-and-slop marina.
Small wet footprints shone on the kitchen lino.
A new view. Below: the casualty entrance,
the neon-lit triage nurse at her counter.
Beyond: black hills wearing necklaces of fire.
It was the twentieth century somewhere
between Mereweather by the Pacific
and One, Paradise Avenue, Mount Pleasant.
Elvis was entering his jumpsuit era.
A newspaper in a half-unpacked tea chest
showed an undrinkable boot-print on the moon.

Having made peace with the dust we depend on
for judging the relative distance of hills
or pointing at stars with powerful spotlights,
my mother was stepping through a proof, but then
she paused to doodle what were still considered
mathematical monsters: fern, cloud, coastline
– self-similar wonderforms inspiralling –
the night her three-dimensional dry-point print.

A Different Party

You missed the *best* night. Guess Who was there. She goes,
Elvis stole Englebert Humperdinck's sideburns.
True or false? And I'm like, So what if he did?
My turn. Spot the common denominator:
water holes mirror the sky eyes flame the mind.
But she was wincing, What do you call that noise?
And I'm like, It only *sounds* repetitive.
The atmosphere was infected with wisecracks
no less malicious for being accurate.
But she goes, Check this peephole installation,
and I'm like, Gaslight, spread legs, waterfall, *what*?
She's like mica flakes spinning in a river.
I'm like a wave-cut platform pocked with rock-pools.

She's like a lipstick shift to a bolder shade,
like operation crimson or sea wind rose.
And I'm like a knot of frayed octopus straps.
She's like a library bust swivelled by a child
to look at what must be a sward, encircled
by shifty, nocturnal trees, while back inside
The Chemical History of a Candle
by Faraday lies open on a table.

A Lead

When the music stops, who's the first to let go
in the dance studio with its rooftop views
of unreconstructed rust and giant tags?
After the series of tactile surprises
(you'd never have predicted just by looking
how wildly successive partners can vary
in temperature, pressure and humidity
of grip), who lets go first? It's invisible
but unmistakable. The class disperses,
the dose of rhythm dissipating, although
its benefits may still be felt days later
in the smoothly gratuitous precision
of an alemana turn on kitchen tiles.

One student is leaving by the fire escape
with its view of resting cranes and sunset rust,
remembering a lead with give and a scent
of smoky saliva, which (all unawares)
promised a world of inventive tenderness
and a way of letting trouble come undone
rather than build or spread (when the argument
is starting again, who's the first to let go?)

One Thing and Another

A snake came flowing out of a dry stone wall.
A man froze. The snake went slithering away.
All its cthonic realm was a hole in the ground.
The man breathed again. He'd been given a room
with a looming wardrobe in the old hotel
behind him, beyond the bed-and-breakfast zone.
How he washed up there was not entirely clear.
He remembered surprising a glance that meant
Welcome to the club of people who have tried
to help him and got burnt (he had to admit,
statistically, it was more than reasonable).
Affective overdrafts. Staggering bathrooms.
The embers of bridge- and boat-timbers fading.

It's one thing to swallow that number of pills
and another to hold them down, thankfully,
and still another to find yourself climbing
a hill pitted by incorrigible hope,
an upended gold dust bowl, discovering
sun-bathed scenes of picturesque abandonment,
the simple rhythms of the wind whistling through
a tram stranded in a paddock of bleached grass.

Face Work

As the wind shifts, habitual states of mind
are gradually written in muscle and skin,
though not as irreversibly as the years.
Or so I hoped on seeing a lived-in face
with an open, mobile but unevasive
weather-filled gaze, quite unlike the slitty peer
that locks onto objects of fear and envy.
Only sort of childlike, because in those eyes
the world was not one big object of wonder
but the intricate mother of all puzzles
riddled with durable gaps to glory in.
Below, the mere ghost of a serious smile
inspired short-lived micro-resolutions:

unclamp your lips; unset your jaw; recover
lost adolescent lower-face positions:
mouth hanging open and bottom lip bitten.
By betraying what you have come to expect
of the world with its roses and gobs of spit,
the face that mirrors mask, that you can only
see in another, is making things happen.
The open may still be deep in it somewhere.

Mottoes

Neither hope nor fear sounds good in theory or
maybe just sad and probably too general
to be much help. How about neither whinging
about how academics keep inventing
ways to feel good about watching bad TV
nor celebrating the subversive tactics
of the fully empowered couch potato.
Neither bagging the know-nothing young who know
the last party sealed a pact and the next one
will be a metaphysical adventure
nor trying to prove you can still dance all night
(the fat bass will stomp on while outside frogs plop
under stars barbaric to a northern eye).

Neither siding with the ugly as they watch
time wreaking their revenge on the beautiful
nor secretly subscribing to the not-so-
archaic belief that bad luck is catching.
Neither rehearsing a charmingly modest
Golden Logie speech nor getting nostalgic
about hiccoughs or the park of a lifetime.
Neither doormat nor systematic cactus.

Zombie Charmers

Don't go thinking we're like the sad guys you use
to test sunny, fun-loving ideas of sex –
So how would you feel about *him* doing it
with your ghost? – whose bluish foreheads are inscribed
with the epitaph of the corporate undead:
He lost his life trying to get a CV.
Whenever you're making a meal of those guys,
we shall be among you. We do jocular
menace: keep laughing or the gloves come off. Look,
it's better all round if we win because we
are seriously bad losers, mate. On campus
we like the word *eliminativism*
and shuddering at the conceptually poor.

Some say we're fabulously implausible
like a pint of stout lighting up the world or
innervated space or a donkey on fire
only more so. But we don't need your belief.
Don't come trying to put yourself in our shoes.
You don't know what it's like and you never will.
We're atom-for-atom duplicates of you
but there's nothing at all it's like to be us.

Tourism (II)

Not a revenant but a dim precursor,
thinking, This is surely a beautiful place,
but how long will it be before I arrive?
A square like a courtyard: millstones in the walls,
tiles, trickling water and a broken column.
Would living in this patrimonial hive
make carscapes with riots of signage designed
to catch a speeding eye exotic or vile?
The millstones are hard. Dark tobacco smoke drifts.
Calamitous history has left its marks
all over the place, and yet somehow it seems
a cunningly animated peep-box scene.
Condemned to confuse the ugly and the real,

or just tired, bumbling around like a zombie
in wonderland, where seagulls and sirens sound
different but familiar from soundtracks, I feel
like an extra in an atmospheric film:
anything could happen and nothing much does.
An old man uses a light-green laundry tank
to locate the leak in his bicycle tube.
Dry oranges hang in the pre-Christmas mist.

Invisible Hinges

If between one footfall and the next, the wind
can swivel and issue empty threats of rain,
for all we know this could be one of those days,
unpinpointable even in retrospect,
when a dimly-held belief begins to melt,
say the belief that it's somehow generous
to assume that everyone's rather like you.
An open-ended day promising nothing,
but just as full of zipjams, language splashes
and thixotropic flows, lost somewhere between
the day you realized you wouldn't always
have to pretend to be interested in X
(opera, hot cars, Buffy Summers, poetry)

and the day when you will blush for the last time.
Although it has no sort of narrative arc
except the fall of promise into fatigue,
a lost day like this could begin to dissolve
the belief that since our time is tight I'm free
to be proud of knowing nothing about Y.
A dithering day I step out of into
a scent of gently exploding roses – gone.

Prop

I prop up the dog and wait for him to pee.
Three a.m. A phrase goes floating through my head:
"A still Prussian-blue night with rather weak stars."
In the dirt where summer scorched the lawn away
a puddle forms, burnt-umber summer that changed
the climate of feeling about climate change.
Weak stars because a fullish moon is climbing
into the sky like scandalous new talent
with no intention of inspiring envy,
climbing above the autumnal pergola
shedding butter- and claret-coloured vine leaves
sprung from a stock gnarled like an arthritic leg,
rotting at the core, propped up with a fence post.

Moonlight makes the puddle's meniscus glisten.
The sky my black cab dripping from the car wash.
The Earth wobbling on through space, riddled with life,
from the thickening mothers of vinegar
to insomniacs anonymous who see
a future of unscheduled meetings with death,
from sap-green bamboo for Shanghai scaffolding
to an old dog running away in his dreams.

The Penultimate

The second-last summer Sunday afternoon.
A dog tottering on his second-last legs
beside a converted traffic barrier
leaking water through a hose to save a tree.
What was diffusely sad at the time now seems
a moment of golden reprieve, now the smell
of that dog is going from the world, although
for a time it will cling to certain fabrics.
And you don't need to tell me that life goes on
seething in its abyssal variety.
Grander and more promising particulars
are always falling away, beyond the reach
of anyone on earth as it is. I know,

as much as I can for the moment, I know.
(The parents of a particular young man
named Maarten keep their phone number in Holland
posted at the base of Volcán Osorno.)
I cross the muddy yard. Airy cages hold
the winter sun. Three claret-coloured leaves still
cling to the vine, and the hoot of a train fools
ears attuned to a sound that meant Help me.

If I Stop

When the unknown feeling from the hinterland
came on the wings of pop, I would shut my eyes,
let the tingling spread over my scalp, and hope
that this time it would last long enough to turn
life inside out, as it must, I felt, one day.
Did I really expect the drab and the cramped
to put on all the panoramic splendour
of dawn observed from the back seat of a car
winding towards an intact beach holiday?
Was it a pure illusion? Is a tremor
less real for having no substance of its own?
Those hints of the unknown would leave me feeling
nostalgic for the next five-second party.

Now that I've learnt a few conceptual moves
("it should be clear I am deeply suspicious")
to keep people off my case, not much has changed.
And if I stop longing for the imminence
of a revelation that hasn't happened
yet, pied butcher birds will sing on regardless;
the mist will lift, the light will sink, the backwash
will go on scooping thigh-deep pools to seaward.

Envoy

Plenty of bottles have sunk to the sea floor
messages slowly dissolving inside them,
others have washed up a short walk down the beach
or far away but a century too late
for the sender, though not for the retiree
archiving items of exotic flotsam.
How many super-durable monuments
are settling on the windscreens of cars in Rome
as I put this together from lines drafted
with a finger in beach sand or a texta
on a tile by anon? This gappy lattice
suddenly crystallizing from a slowly
enriched solution of possibilities

would have to be further up itself than Oz-
ymandias to pose as a monument,
but it's brazen enough to hope that someone
might take a piece for another mosaic,
as you might pick up a sanded glass pebble,
a piece of this perishable instrument
in two hundred and thirty-one syllables.
So get out, little poem, go on, get lost.

Notes on the Text

The "four billion streams of human experience" in "A Theory of Next Thursday Night" are borrowed from a sentence in the introduction to Galen Strawson's *Mental Reality*.

"Paradise" incorporates a line from one of Tennyson's suppressed poems, "The Mystic" ("Time flowing in the middle of the night"), and a line from a lost poem by Thomas Lovell Beddoes, remembered by Thomas Kelsall and quoted by John Ashbery in *Other Traditions* ("Like the red outline of beginning Adam").

A Note About the Author

Chris Andrews was born in Newcastle (Australia) in 1962. He grew up in Melbourne. After completing a Ph.D at the University of Melbourne, he taught there, in the French department, from 1995 to 2008. In 2009 he took up a position at the University of Western Sydney, where he is a member of the Writing and Society Research Centre. His first book of poems was *Cut Lunch* (Indigo, 2002). He has translated books of fiction by Latin American authors, including Roberto Bolaño's *By Night in Chile* (Harvill / New Directions, 2003) and César Aira's *Varamo* (New Directions, 2012), and was a recipient of the Vallé-Inclan Prize for Literary Translation from Spanish (British Society of Authors) (2005).

A Note About the Anthony Hecht Poetry Prize

The Anthony Hecht Poetry Prize was inaugurated in 2005 and is awarded on an annual basis to the best first or second collection of poems submitted.

2005
Judge: J. D. McClatchy
Winner: Morrie Creech, *Field Knowledge*

2006
Judge: Mary Jo Salter
Winner: Erica Dawson, *Big-Eyed Afraid*

2007
Judge: Richard Wilbur
Winner: Rose Kelleher, *Bundle o' Tinder*

2008
Judge: Alan Shapiro
Winner: Carrie Jerrell, *After the Revival*

2009
Judge: Rosanna Warren
Winner: Matthew Ladd, *The Book of Emblems*

2010
Judge: James Fenton
Winner: Mark Kraushaar, *The Uncertainty Principle*

2011
Judge: Mark Strand
Winner: Chris Andrews, *Lime Green Chair*

For further information, please visit Waywiser's website at

http://waywiser-press.com/hechtprize.html